MW01092758

Woman to Woman

How to Start, Grow, and Maintain a Mentoring Ministry

MENTORING

Mentee Handbook

JANET THOMPSON

LifeWay Press
Nashville, Tennessee

ISBN 0-6330-0288-7

Dewey Decimal Classification: 248.843

Subject Heading: WOMEN\CHURCH WORK WITH WOMEN

Unless otherwise noted, Scripture quotations are from the Holy Bible,
New International Version, copyright © 1973, 1978, 1984 by International Bible Society

To order additional copies of this resource: WRITE LifeWay Church Resources Customer Service,
127 Ninth Avenue, North; Nashville, TN 37234-0113; FAX (615) 251-5933;
PHONE 1-800-458-2772; EMAIL *customerservice@lifeway.com;*
order ONLINE at *www.lifeway.com*; or visit the LifeWay Christian Store serving you.

For information about adult discipleship and family resources, training, and events,
visit our Web site at *www.lifeway.com/discipleplus.*

Printed in the United States of America

LifeWay Press
127 Ninth Avenue, North
Nashville, Tennessee 37234-0151

*As God works through us, we will help people and churches
know Jesus Christ and seek His kingdom by providing biblical solutions
that spiritually transform individuals and cultures.*

Contents

About the Author

JANET THOMPSON is the founder and director of AHW Ministries, also known as About His Work Ministries. In addition to her work as an author and speaker on topics relevant to today's Christian women, Janet has been "about His work" as a lay minister starting and leading the Woman to Woman Mentoring Ministry at Saddleback Church in Lake Forest, California. The Woman to Woman Mentoring Ministry was founded in January 1996 and continues to grow as hundreds of women experience the blessings of becoming Titus 2 women.

In order to share the Saddleback Church ministry with other churches, Janet wrote and self-published the kit, *Woman to Woman: How to Start, Grow, and Maintain a Mentoring Ministry*. As hundreds of churches used the original kit to start mentoring ministries, thousands of women around the world committed to walk beside each other in woman to woman mentoring relationships.

Janet has a Bachelor of Science degree in Food Administration from California Polytechnic University, a Masters degree in Business Administration from California Lutheran University, and a Master of Arts degree in Christian Leadership from Fuller Theological Seminary. She is also a CLASS (Christian Leaders, Authors and Speakers) graduate.

The Lord has blessed Janet with many life experiences. Janet and her husband, Dave, have four children and three grandchildren. They are now enjoying the season of life known as the empty nest or, as Janet calls it, "parent's time to rest." Dave is a manufacturer's representative in the golf industry and a helpmate/partner with Janet in AHW Ministries. They make their home in Lake Forest, California.

Janet's Thoughts to the Mentee

Congratulations! You are about to embark on an experience that will change your life and the lives of all those around you. It is not just your mentor who is going to change your life. It is the Lord working through her and your new mentoring relationship. I know it is thrilling to have a Christian woman in your life who cares about you and wants to help you achieve your full potential in Christ. Always remember, though, that she is still human, just like you. She is the vessel that the Lord is choosing to work through at this time in your life to accomplish His great work; just as the Lord used me as a vessel to start Woman to Woman Mentoring.

On April 25, 1995, the Lord spoke clearly to me while I was attending a Women in Ministry Conference. I heard in my mind and heart, "Feed My sheep." I said, "OK" even though I had no idea who the sheep were or what I would feed them when I found them.

The next day, the workshop leader began her talk with John 21:15-17 where Jesus tells Peter, "If you love me, go and feed my sheep." Her topic was shepherding women in your church. I knew very few women in my church, and I had never participated in women's ministry. I knew He was answering the question of who the sheep were, but I still did not understand how I was going to feed them. Two weeks later, when Emmie, an acquaintance at work, first asked me to be her mentor I was flattered, but cautious. I had no idea what mentoring meant, but I did think that perhaps she was the "sheep" and mentoring might just be the "feeding." A friend of my daughter also asked me to mentor her. I had never met Kristen before she asked me to be her mentor. Kristen was only 21 at the time. How could she possibly want me to mentor her? But she did, and so I did. I thought I had now fulfilled my call to feed His sheep. Then one of the pastors at my church told me about all the young women in the young adults group that were asking for a mentor.

That was my first clue that younger women really wanted to learn from older women. I had always tried to be out of the house when my daughter had her Bible study. However, one night when she could not be there to lead it, she asked me to sub for her. I said I would be happy to, but I was not sure if the girls would come. We had 100 percent attendance that night, and the girls asked me if I would continue meeting with them as the senior advisor in the group. They liked that I was willing to share my life experiences with them. It also helped that I knew some of the history of the 60s and 70s which interested them. That is how I happened to be there the night Kristen visited the group and, as we were talking later in the evening, she asked me if I would mentor her.

I believe the Lord used Kristen and Emmie to spur my interest in learning about mentoring. I thought in the beginning that it would just be for them. Little did I know that He had *you* in mind

also. Churches are full of women who are new in the Lord and are looking for someone to show them how to live the life of a Christian woman today.

I suddenly realized that "feed My sheep" meant more than just Emmie and Kristen. There were many sheep, and I was only one mentoring shepherd. The rest is history, and you are a part of that history. With the birth of the Woman to Woman Mentoring Ministry at Saddleback Church, hundreds of women began to experience the benefits of a one-on-one mentoring experience.

But that was just at Saddleback Church. The Lord had even more sheep in mind for me to feed. The *Woman to Woman: How to Start, Grow, and Maintain a Mentoring Ministry Kit* was first made available in May 1997. By October 1997, 120 churches throughout the United States, Canada, and Germany had obtained the kit to start a Mentoring Ministry in their churches. More sheep–lots of feeding. Today there are hundreds of churches and thousands of sheep!

Why do I tell you this story? Because I want you to know that you are not alone in your desire to be mentored. The Lord knew that today you would be in this mentoring relationship, and He used me to facilitate that for you. You are part of the plan He has for women to reach out to each other, reunite, and share the knowledge and wisdom that can only come with the experience that age brings. In your Christian mentor, you have age in the Lord. She may not be that much older than you chronologically, but she is spiritually older.

As you grow in spiritual maturity, the Lord will use you someday as a mentor, also. You will want to give back just as someone has given to you. It may not be for quite awhile, or it could happen after this relationship ends. Remember that if you are one day old in the Lord, you are older than someone who just gave her life to Christ. Don't rush it, but always be thinking about how you can serve from what you have learned.

You have no idea how many other lives will be touched besides those of you and your mentor. I can tell you story after story of marriages saved, families restored, relationships mended, illnesses going into remission, depression turning to joy, and emotional and spiritual healing that have resulted from two women committing to spend six months in a mentoring relationship. Most of the time these were two women who did not even know each other before being matched.

Two women, not known to each other, but well known by God. He knows just who to match together to fulfill the plans He has for each of you. Having someone to give you God's perspective on your situation will do what no marriage counselor, attorney, or doctor can. It will help you go to the one and only Counselor, Prince of Peace, and Great Physician. And what does this take on your part? Your time, energy, and love, and you will get the same back tenfold. Enjoy your mentoring experience as you go—About His Work.

Blessings,

Janett Thompson

Lord, I Want to Be a Good Mentee

Where do you start? In prayer. You cannot be a good mentee on your own. None of us can. The only hope we have at any measure of success is to hand the entire mentoring relationship over to Him—not once, but daily. Every morning in your quiet time, pray that you will be humble and open to what He wants you to learn in your mentoring relationship.

Mentoring will always be a two-way relationship in more aspects than you can possibly imagine at this time. Do not ever feel as if you are doing all the taking, because your mentor is going to be receiving, also. There will be times when she is having a bad day or maybe even a crisis in her life, and it will be comforting to her to know that she can share it with you and receive your prayers. All of us benefit from having a friend that we can trust to share the joys and sorrows of our lives. The servant will also be served. I wish that I could talk with each and every one of you after your mentoring experience to see how God worked in your life during this time.

1. Humbleness

It does take a certain degree of humility to seek wise counsel and teaching from someone else. However, dying to the old self and taking on the new life in Christ is all about humility. As new Christians, we humbly admit that we have sinned and done wrong and ask for Christ's forgiveness. Then as we begin to live this exciting new life, we all must admit that we need guidance and direction in how to live a life that is free of our old sinful ways.

Hand the entire

mentoring relationship

over to Him—

not once, but daily.

2. Openness

Openness, along with a willingness to be vulnerable, is essential to a mentoring relationship. In order for a mentoring relationship to be fruitful, you will need to seek out a level of trust with your mentor. You want to feel that you can share with her the areas where you would like to grow and perhaps even be held accountable. Of course, this will take time. She will have to earn that trust from you.

3. Honesty

This coincides with candidness. If you are going to have a relationship that is meaningful, you will both need to be honest with each other. If something is not comfortable for you, let your mentor know. Do not expect that she will be able to guess what is on your mind.

4. Adaptability

You must have a willingness to learn. Growth is about moving forward, learning new ways, and in some cases changing old ways that no longer serve us well. Your mentor may show you new ways of doing things as a Christian. It could be a step of putting off the old and putting on the new, and that can sometimes be difficult and even painful. "You were taught, with regard to your former way of life, to put off your old self, which is being corrupted by its deceitful desires; to be made new in the attitude of your minds; and to put on the new self, created to be like God in true righteousness and holiness" (Eph. 4:22-24).

Maximizing Your Mentoring Experience

DEVELOP SPIRITUAL HABITS

I use the word *habit* rather than *discipline* because discipline sounds so painful. Habits can be bad such as a drug habit, but they can also be something good that you do habitually or routinely in your life. You may have bad habits you would like to eliminate, and you are hoping that this mentoring relationship will accomplish that. I hope so, too.

Remember, though, that your mentor cannot rid you of the old and bring the new good habits into your life. She can talk to you about these habits and encourage you, but only you, with the help of the Holy Spirit, can take the steps to incorporate positive changes into your life. However, following spiritual habits will help you grow in your Christian walk, as well as receive so much more from your mentoring relationship. The Lord speaks to us in many ways, and your mentor will be one of the vehicles He uses. He also longs for you to develop the habit of listening and talking to Him through:

- Praying
- Having a daily quiet time
- Attending church regularly
- Fellowshipping with other Christians
- Reading books written by Christian authors
- Seeking wise counsel from your pastors and other Christian authorities

Praying: First, pray that the Lord will give you courage and receptiveness to the role your mentor will play in your life. Thank the Lord for the opportunity to receive wisdom from a godly woman. That is something to be cherished. Following is a prayer you might want to pray for both her and you.

The Lord speaks to us
in many ways,
and your mentor
will be one of the
vehicles He uses.

Mentee's Prayer

Lord, I know that You have led me to seek a mentor because You want me to grow in my Christian walk. You want me to learn from a role model who is living the type of life You want for me. Lord, help me to be receptive to the changes I might need to make, and humble enough to admit that there are things I need to learn.

Lord, please give me patience when I feel frustrated, love when I feel angry, grace when I want to condemn, mercy when I want to judge, courage when I want to avoid, hope when I think it will never change, perseverance when I want to give up, acceptance when I feel rejected, clarity when I feel misunderstood, discernment to detect right from wrong when I am confused, humility when I think I can do it on my own.

You have led me to seek a mentor, now let me be receptive to what it is You want me to learn from her. Help me to be open and eager to learn more about You and Your ways. I want to be a godly woman who conducts herself in a way that pleases You. I want to become more familiar with Your ways and what it means to be a servant of Christ.

Help me to be considerate of the mentor You have brought to me. Let me remember that she gives to me selflessly, and I need to be respectful of her time and energy. Let me be a blessing to her in return. Father, I thank You in advance for the plans You have for me, and I am grateful that You have put this desire to learn more about You and Your ways on my heart.

Please give me energy, time, wisdom, knowledge, compassion, understanding, faith, and hope. Help me to always be a survivor and not a victim. Fill me, Lord, with the Holy Spirit, and let me honor You in all that I say and do each day. Amen.

The words in this prayer come from my heart and from being a mentor myself. I know all the feelings and fears that can arise, along with the joys and miracles of a mentoring relationship. Give your relationship to God daily and then get ready to receive the blessings of this new relationship.

If praying is something you would like to learn more about, tell your mentor you would like the enhancement of your prayer life to be one of the goals of your relationship. Praying out loud may be difficult for you. Do not be embarrassed to talk to her about it and ask for her support in helping you become more comfortable in this area of your prayer life. It is a very common apprehension. Your mentor would be a perfect person to practice on. Just have a conversation with God and her. That is all prayer is—conversation with God.

Something else that might help you in the area of prayer is using a prayer journal. Use the Prayer and Praise Journal form located in the Appendix of your handbooks (you have permission to duplicate this page for your personal use) or use a journal of your own. You and your mentor can keep your journals together, and you will see the Lord working in and through you both. Bring your handbooks and journals to your meetings.

Having a daily quiet time: Next, you need to have a daily quiet time where you pray and talk to God, read your Bible, and perhaps do a Bible study. A quiet time is essential to the Christian life and the Christian seeking wisdom. You need your time with God, especially when you are wanting to learn more about Him and grow in your spiritual walk. You cannot go about your day serving Him, if you have not even checked in with Him in the morning to see what it is He wants you to do that day.

If you do not have an established quiet time—start one. There are numerous books, devotionals, and journals available to make it more structured if you prefer, and I give you some suggestions in the "Books That I Recommend" section of the Appendix. This would be another good goal for your relationship and perhaps an area where you would like to be held accountable.

Attending church: This is a given for a Christian woman. You need feeding at least weekly, and you need to be among the family of God. A vital part of the Christian life is sharing it with others and learning from those inspired to preach. There is nothing to compare with lifting your voice to the Lord with other believers and praying together.

This is something you might do with your mentor, if that fits your schedules. Many mentoring relationships like to attend midweek services together. This is usually more of a Bible study and more informal. You can go out for coffee after and discuss the message. As Christians, our calling is to use our God-given gifts and talents to uplift and build the body of Christ. Perhaps you and your mentor could explore areas where you could serve your church together. A great way to start is in the mentoring ministry itself.

Fellowshipping with other Christians: You need to be fellowshipping among Christian friends in addition to your mentor. You and she will have a scheduled time together each week. However, being around others who are spiritually mature will help you grow in your walk and become wiser in your ways. This might be in your small group, women's Bible study, or just time you spend socializing together. Always be open to listening and learning.

Reading books written by Christian authors: Your mentor cannot possibly be an authority on every area of life. But there are many resources that both you and she can access. There is a book by a Christian author on almost any topic imaginable that we as women encounter. Many things in our lives we think should not happen to Christians, and there are books written on those, too. Making the time to read is an invaluable source of growth and maturity, emotionally and intellectually. Your church, or even the mentoring ministry, may have a library where you can check out books if finances do not let you purchase them. I really encourage sharing among the body of Christ, and we need to all make our resources available to each other.

Christian authors who feel called by God to share our knowledge and experience do not write just to help ourselves. We write to make that information or life experience God has given us available to others to learn and grow from. So take advantage of it.

Seeking wise counsel from your pastors and other Christian authorities: Other ways to seek knowledge and wisdom are to consult with pastors at your church or use your Bible concordance to look up topics in question. Search out Bible verses in which the Lord gives you His perspective on the situation. Talk to Christian authorities, and in some cases you may need to seek Christian counseling or make an appointment with someone who is skilled in the areas under question.

While the mentor

takes responsibility

for the relationship,

it cannot be a success

without your

participation

and enthusiasm.

PRACTICAL TIPS ON BEING A MENTEE

Remember that the relationship is always a two-way relationship and your role in ensuring its success is vital. While the mentor takes responsibility for the relationship, it cannot be a success without your participation and enthusiasm. There are specific things you can do that will help keep your relationship consistent and maximize its potential for both of you. Just as in any relationship, communicating and taking time for each other will be key factors in ensuring an ongoing and dynamic mentoring relationship.

Here are several tips for you as the mentee:

- Participate in setting goals in the beginning for your relationship. Let your mentor know the areas you would like to focus on. Use the suggestions on page 25.
- Return all her phone calls within 24 hours, if possible.
- Do not cancel or reschedule appointments unless it is an emergency.
- Take your calendar to every meeting with your mentor.
- Be flexible in adjusting your schedule to determine meeting times.
- If you have children, make arrangements to not have them with you when you meet.
- Be respectful of your mentor's time. She is not on-call or available 24 hours a day.

• Always remember to ask how she is doing, and if she has any prayer requests.

Setting Goals

Set goals early in your relationship. The suggestions on page 25 of this handbook, "How to Set Creative Goals for Your M&M Relationship," were developed by a mentor and mentee. Use them. I cannot stress enough the importance of goal setting. No goals–no direction–no focus–no time–no interest–no relationship. That, unfortunately, can be the direction of a relationship without goals. You will probably be the one that gives direction to the relationship. For example, are there areas of accountability or special support you feel you need help with? When your mentor asks you where you want to focus the relationship, be prepared to give her your thoughts. Pray about this before your first meeting.

If you are a new Christian, you will want to know how to get started learning and growing in Christ, and receive direction in living this new life. If you have recently rededicated your life, you will probably want to review and renew your knowledge of the Bible and ask for support in not falling back into the areas where you backslid before.

If you have been a Christian for awhile and want to continue growing and becoming stronger in the Lord, you might want to do a Bible study or have more of a discipleship relationship. Many people ask me the difference between *discipling* and *mentoring*. Dr. Ted W. Engstrom explains it well in his book, *The Fine Art of Mentoring,* where he makes the following distinction.

" 'Discipling' is a close synonym, with these differences: A discipler is one who helps an understudy to

     1. give up his own will for the will of God the Father,

     2. live daily a life of spiritual sacrifice for the glory of Christ, and

     3. strive to be consistently obedient to the commands of his Master.

A mentor, on the other hand, provides modeling, close supervision on special projects, individual help in many areas—discipline, encouragement, correction, confrontation, and a calling to accountability."[1]

Another option I give for the focus in your relationship is accountability. If that is to be your focus, you need to discuss this very carefully and thoroughly with your mentor. Be sure that you make clear to her:

• the areas where you want accountability;

• how you want to be held accountable;

• ways in which you will agree to being held accountable.

You will need to give your agreement and permission for your mentor to work with you on areas where you ask for help. Your mentor will ask you to *formally* agree to being held accountable, and to help establish how and when she will do it. Then you will want to be receptive and accepting when occasions arise where she will need to ask you questions or point out to you the areas where there is still need for improvement.

Do not ask for accountability unless you genuinely want it and know that you can accept it without feeling defensive or angry. Your mentor will talk to you in love, but if you have asked for frankness, then you will want to pray about being able to receive it. There may be times she will need to tell you something that you really do not want to hear. Be sure you both pray together before this type of discussion. Accountability is an appropriate role for your mentor. However, if she does not feel capable of dealing with the issues where you need accountability, she may tell you that and advise you to seek out a Christian professional.

Bobb Biehl and Glen Urquhart point out that, "It is important to remember that all accountability is ultimately to God. Just because a mentor will let you get by with something does not mean that God will. Just because a mentor feels something is okay does not mean that God does. Just because you can successfully hide something from the mentor who is holding you accountable does not mean it is hidden from God.

"Just so, a mentor is not to be held accountable for the protégé's success. The mentor can help the protégé succeed in reaching his or her goals, but the responsibility for reaching goals always remains clearly with the protégé."[2]

The main reason for accountability is to help you reach spiritual maturity and to develop your full potential as a Christian woman. It can be a very vital benefit of your relationship, if discussed and prayed about by both of you and kept in the context and perspective of the mentoring relationship goals.

Scheduling Time Together

Consistent meetings are essential to the success and growth of your mentoring relationship. You can have great goals and fabulous intentions, but if you are not meeting to discuss them and interact with each other, they are pointless. You need to take an active role in assuring that the meetings take place.

Make your meeting times a priority on your calendar and in your life. You stepped out and asked for a mentor, now it is important that you take the second step and fit it into your probably-already-overbooked schedule. We all make time for things that are important to us, so be sure to adjust your schedule to incorporate this new important relationship.

In the Kickoff Night section of this handbook, I have listed ways to make this easier for you. Many precious moments are wasted playing telephone tag. To stay consistent, take your calendar with you to each meeting and schedule your next meeting before you leave. Then do not change it unless there is an emergency. This also gives you time to arrange for your children if that is necessary. Remember that your mentor is doing the same thing. She is planning her schedule around your times together. Let her know that you value her and her time. Be considerate in making adjustments that are necessary on both your parts to reach a mutually agreeable meeting time.

Being Respectful of Your Mentor's Time

Keep in mind that your mentor is serving you and the Lord and giving freely of her time. Rescheduling and canceling can play havoc in her life. If she has made time in her schedule to meet with you for a certain time, keep to that time frame. Unless she has told you to call her anytime, remember that she has obligations and is not going to be an on-call mentor. If you have specific needs that require that kind of support, you may need to arrange for additional Christian assistance in those areas.

I know you would never expect this, but unless she offers, baby-sitting or filling in for an absent grandmother to your children is not appropriate. While she will be a friend to the whole family, this is specifically a relationship between you and her. You both need to agree to anything beyond that.

Asking Questions and Seeking Solutions to Problems

If you have a question or problem, first check "Frequently Asked Questions and Suggested Answers" in the Appendix of this handbook. You may find the advice and answer you seek there. If not, call your **Prayer Warrior** or the **Ministry Relations Shepherdess**, or the designated person in your ministry. Do not wait until your mentoring relationship is in trouble. Get help right away. The relationship can never fail unless you both give up on it. As long as you stay committed and faithful to your part of the Mentoring Covenant, there is hope for it to mend.

Your mentor is a godly woman who has stepped forward to share her life and experiences with you.

UNDERSTAND THE ROLE OF YOUR MENTOR

What can you expect from your mentor? That is a good question, and I am glad you asked it. It is important to remember that your mentor is not a professional mentor. She is a godly woman in your church who has stepped forward to share her life and experiences with you. Titus 2:3-5 tells the older women in the church to be Christian mentors. The Titus 2 woman, as she is often called, is to set the example and role model of what a woman following Christ in her daily life looks like, acts like, talks like, relates like, works like, loves like.

The difference between just being a role model and being a mentor is that you can admire role models from afar and pattern your life after them, but you may never know them personally. A mentor is someone who takes an interest in your life and cares about you. It is a personal relationship. A Christian mentoring relationship has a common ground of being sisters in Christ.

On Kickoff Night you will go over the details of what you can and cannot expect from your mentor. I would like to address a couple of those in detail because I want you to have realistic expectations for your mentor. Oswald Chambers wrote in his daily devotional, *My Utmost for His Highest*: "The moral miracle of redemption is that God can put a new nature into me through which I can live a totally new life. But I must get to that point. God cannot put into me, the responsible moral person that I am, the nature that was in Jesus Christ unless I am aware of my need for it."[3]

You are aware of this need in your life, and that is why you came to the Orientation Coffee seeking a mentor. By opening yourself up to godly guidance, you are reaching out and seeking for the "nature that was in Jesus Christ" to come into your own life. What an honor it is for your mentor to be the woman that helps you with your growth in Christ.

Helping you grow in Christ will be her chief function as a mentor in your life. You may have come into the relationship with problems or major challenges and be seeking someone who will have all the answers for you or who can help put parts of your life back together again. Your mentor is not the person who can do that. She can, however, direct you to the One who can, and she can actually accompany your appointments with Him. Of course, I am speaking of Jesus our Lord. He is the Great Healer, Physician, Counselor, and Comforter. He really does have all the answers. The focus for a Christian mentoring relationship is to learn how to take our problems and challenges and put them at the foot of the cross. To look into the Life Manual that has all the answers–the Bible.

The home you grew up in may not have been Christian. If it was not, you did not see a Christian wife, mother, career woman, single woman, sister, aunt, or daughter-in-law role modeled for you as you were growing up. Now, as a Christian woman yourself, you have questions about how to be a Christian woman today. That is where your mentor can help, advise, and model for you. While she will not replace your blood relatives, she can be a spiritual mom to you and guide and teach you the ways of a Christian woman.

This may be all you need to progress in your life. However, there may be some deeper issues that a Christian professional could help you with. Please do not be offended if she suggests that to you. Your mentor received training to not go beyond a boundary she does not feel equipped or capable to handle. She needs to be able to tell you if she feels that is happening.

Assuming the role of a mentor is a big job, but your mentor has said that she is up to it and most importantly is excited and eager to help make this an experience that you will both remember fondly.

STAY FOCUSED ON YOUR RELATIONSHIP WITH GOD

The more you focus on your own relationship with God, the better mentee you are going to become. He will guide you and give the direction and answers that you seek. In all relationships, if we keep our eyes on God instead of another person, we become more like the Lord. That is what being a Christian is all about—relationships—and we know it starts with our relationship with Christ. When we are in tune with our Great Mentor, we become more and more like Him.

I close this section with an excerpt from a devotional I am writing called *Lunch with Jesus*. I share this poem with you as you now prepare to allow your mentor to use her life experiences in helping you develop this wonderful "Life Made New." You might want to share this with your mentor at one of your first meetings.

*A LIFE MADE NEW

On May 11, 1996, I was the speaker at a Saddleback Church women's fellowship gathering called Heart to Heart Cafe. My topic was: A Cup of Encouragement. I talked about the need women have for companionship and mentoring relationships with each other. I gave my own testimony and used it to depict how I might not have backslidden if there had been Christian women mentoring me. I also discussed how at that time I did not perceive a need for women in my life. Frankly, I had not wanted to make the time for women friends, and so I found myself very lonely through many of the trials of being a single parent.

I then shared with the women the numerous miracles the Lord had worked in my life to get me where I was today—initiating and leading a Woman to Woman Mentoring Ministry at Saddleback Church. I was the least likely person the Lord would use, but He knew what was behind my hardened heart better than I did. The blessings that have come out of this awakening are so much fun to share. I also talked about ways that we, as Christian women, could encourage each other on a daily basis and follow the scriptural mandate of Titus 2:3-5, which tells us that one generation of Christian believers shall teach and guide the next generation of believers.

After the talk, I went out to lunch with my neighbor who had accompanied me that day as my guest. My neighbor is from Croatia and had only been in America for five years. She told me that in her country women do not have microwaves, clothes dryers, convenience and frozen foods, and many of them work outside the home until 6:00 p.m. in the evening.

However, she added, "They always have time for their family and friends. Croatia moves at a much slower pace—everything is not so rush-rush. If you call your friend, she tells you to come on over. You may stir her stew while she is ironing (they iron everything because they have no dryers), but you will enjoy a great visit and cup of coffee."

My neighbor said in America if she calls a friend and asks if she can come to visit, she might hear, "Oh, I really don't have time. I have a nail and tanning salon appointment, then I have to go to the chiropractor, pick up the clothes at the cleaners, go to the gym, and see my counselor. Maybe next time." She said after this happened to her several times, she quit calling her friends for a visit.

I came home from lunch and wrote the poem, "A Life Made New."

A Life Made New

They say I have the gift to speak,
And yet you know how hard I worked.
The hours I practiced, the loss of sleep,
Yet the next engagement is already booked.

I have a message straight from You,
And I know You want the story told,
It's all about a life made new
That needs to be heard by the young and old.

Where will I get the energy?
I find myself asking out loud.
Yet I know you'll be there when I'm on my knees,
Assuring me that I'll do you proud.

The women of today are lonely.
They've built their walls so high.
This wasn't what you meant by holy,
But we have made your words apply.

What happened to the coffee klatch?
The chats as we hung out clothes to dry?
Our modern lives have us so on the dash,
We have to schedule time to cry.

How can we slow them down?
What would You have me say?
To help replace their frown
With smiles and laughter and time to pray.

We need each other can't they see;
That a woman's intuition knows just what to say
When we've lost our joy and there is no peace,
And we can't seem to face yet another day.

The women of today would say,
"Life's different now, there is no time."
If we could talk to those of yesterday,
I think they'd say, "that's such a crime."

We need each other. Only women can
Comprehend the uniqueness of our womanhood.
That's why You made us different from man,
And we'll never be happy till that's understood.

We are a chosen generation
You have a plan for everyone.
Women were your inspiration.
You wanted to make the world more fun.

I guess we'll have to persevere,
Just me and You;
Until all the women come to hear
The story of a life made new.

Janet Thompson 5/11/96
*Excerpt from *Lunch with Jesus*

[1] Bobb Biehl and Glen Urquhart, *Mentoring: How to Find a Mentor–How to Become One* (Colorado Springs, CO: Focus on the Family, 1994), 5.

[2] Ibid., 11.

[3] This material is taken from *My Utmost for His Highest* by Oswald Chambers, edited by James Reimann, copyright © 1992 by Oswald Chambers Publications Assn., Ltd. Original edition copyright © 1935 by Dodd Mead & Co., renewed 1963 by the Oswald Chambers Publications Assn., Ltd., and is used by permission of Discovery House Publishers, Box 3566, Grand Rapids, MI 49501. All rights reserved.

Kickoff Night

Agenda for Kickoff Night

7:00 p.m.

   1. Welcome to mentors

   2. Opening prayer

   3. Distribute *Woman to Woman Mentoring: Mentor* and *Mentee Handbooks*

   4. "With God's Help You Can Be a Mentor"

   5. Mentor Training: "Thoughts for the Mentor"

   6. Announce date for Mentor Halftime Refresher _____

   7. Question and answer time

   8. Pass out Profile Cards

8:30-8:45 p.m.

   9. Break: Mentees arrive and are greeted by their mentors

8:45-9:00 p.m.

   10. Welcome mentees and pray

   11. Mentee Training: "Ways to Get the Most Out of Your Mentoring Relationship as a Mentee"

   12. Discuss Mentoring Convenants and commitments

   13. Review Areas of Opportunity for Service

   14. Announce date of Six-Month Potluck Celebration _____

   15. Introduce Prayer Warriors who will be praying and calling once a month

9:00-10:00 p.m.

   16. Mentors and mentees sign Covenants; Prayer Warriors witness and pray

   17. M&Ms get acquainted

   18. At 9:45 Prayer Warriors meet and pray with assigned M&Ms as a group

   19. Hugs as ladies leave; collect Profile Cards

Kickoff Night Training Lesson

WAYS TO GET THE MOST OUT OF YOUR MENTORING RELATIONSHIP AS A MENTEE

• Are you: Scared? Nervous? Excited? Curious? Well, guess what—your mentor is probably all of those and more. Let's talk about how we can make this the relationship that God planned for each of you.

Remember that your mentor was handpicked by God just for you. There are skills and talents that she has, and only He knows exactly how they will benefit you. To understand better the role of a mentor in your life, we need to look at what she realistically can and cannot be for you.

1. WHAT CAN YOU EXPECT YOUR MENTOR TO BE TO YOU?
   • A godly role model
   • A confidante
   • A listener
   • A prayer partner
   • A Christian friend
   • An encourager
   • An adviser, not an authority
   • Someone to do ministry with
   • A sister in Christ
   • An accountability partner
   • Someone to give a Christian perspective

2. WHAT CAN YOU NOT EXPECT YOUR MENTOR TO BE TO YOU?
   • Your earthly mom or her replacement—she can be a "spiritual mom."
   • A fixer—she will not be able to make everything right in your life.
   • She will not make choices for you. She may give you advice, but you will still make your own choices and take responsibility for those choices.
   • A professional counselor.
   • A Bible scholar (although she will probably be quite knowledgeable).

- Available 24 hours a day.
- Your "best" friend. This will be far more than just a friendship, although that is certainly an element of it.
- She may need to give you a perspective you do not like.
- She will not have the answer to all your problems, but she can direct you to the One who does.
- A woman with a "perfect" life. She will have challenges, too.

3. How Do We keep the relationship going beyond Kickoff Night?
   A. What do you think is the most important factor?

   _____ _____.

   If you are not meeting, there is no relationship! Regular meetings are essential to a successful and meaningful mentoring experience.

   - Coordinating times may be difficult, but never give up on trying to find a compatible date and time.
   - The ideal is the same day and time every week.
   - If your schedules will not allow you to have the same day and time every week, always bring your calendars when you meet and schedule the next meeting time before you leave. This eliminates time spent playing phone tag and weeks where you do not meet. It keeps you both organized.
   - Most people overbook. Make your meetings a commitment and priority for you both. Try not to regularly reschedule.
   - Early morning can sound gruesome, but it works. It keeps you consistent. There are very few scheduling conflicts early in the morning. It really gets your morning started right.
   - Never let more than two weeks go by without meeting unless there is an illness or someone is on vacation.
   - Do not let your mentor feel that you are too busy to meet or talk to her. The Lord will bless your time, and you will get everything accomplished He feels is important.
   - Return calls from your mentor and **Prayer Warrior** in a timely fashion.

4. Questions about your relationship?
   First, look in the Appendix of this handbook at the "Frequently Asked Questions and Suggested Answers" and see if there is a suggestion there that helps. If not, call your **Prayer Warrior** or leave a message on the Mentoring Ministry Information Line.

5. Spiritual or biblical questions?

Suggested Bible Studies to Do Together

Women's Studies:

Becoming a Woman of Excellence by Cynthia Heald

Becoming a Woman of Prayer by Cynthia Heald

Becoming a Woman of Purpose by Cynthia Heald

The Friendships of Women Workbook by Dee Brestin

In My Father's House: Women Relating to God as Father by Mary Kassian

The Joy of Women's Friendships: Sharing the Gift of Intimacy by Dee Brestin

Life Lessons from Women in the Bible by Rhonda Kelley

Living Beyond Yourself: Exploring the Fruit of the Spirit by Beth Moore

Loving Your Husband: Building an Intimate Marriage in a Fallen World by Cynthia Heald

The Virtuous Woman: Shattering the Superwoman Myth by Vicki Courtney

What Every Mom Needs: Balancing Your Life by Elisa Morgan and Carol Kuykendall

A Woman of Joy: 8 Studies from 1, 2, and 3 John by Dee Brestin

Woman to Woman: Preparing Yourself to Mentor by Edna Ellison and Tricia Scribner

Women Connecting with Women: Equipping Women for Friend-to-Friend Support and Mentoring
    by Verna Birkey (This is a book and separate study guide.)

Other studies:

Disciple's Prayer Life by T.W. Hunt and Catherine Walker

Experiencing God: Knowing and Doing the Will of God by Henry Blackaby and Claude King

In God's Presence: Your Daily Guide to a Meaningful Prayer Life by T.W. Hunt and Claude V. King

The Kingdom Agenda: Experiencing God in Your Workplace by Mike and Debi Rogers

Living God's Word: Practical Lessons for Applying Scripture to Life by Waylon B. Moore

My Identity in Christ by Gene Wilkes

When God Speaks: How to Recognize God's Voice and Respond in Obedience
    by Henry Blackaby and Richard Blackaby

*To order these resources WRITE LifeWay Church Resources Customer Service, 127 Ninth Avenue, North, Nashville, TN 37234-0113; FAX (615) 251-5933; PHONE 1-800-458-2772; EMAIL to *CustomerService@lifeway.com*; order ONLINE at *www.lifeway.com*; or visit the LifeWay Christian Store serving you.

How to Set Creative Goals for Your M&M Relationship

1. *Brainstorm:* Write down all the goals, desires, wishes, and dreams you have for yourself. Keep writing until you have exhausted all your thoughts and ideas and are tired of writing. Set your list aside. Pray about it. Return to the list later and make any additions or changes.

2. *Prioritize your goals and ideas:* Go back to your list of goals and read them carefully. Compliment yourself for all your wonderful ideas. Prioritize your goals by numbering them in their order of importance to you.

3. *Share goals:* Share your goals with your mentor at one of your first meetings after Kickoff Night. She will also have a list of goals. Look at your individual lists and see if there are any goals common to both of your lists. Circle them. If there are numerous ones, agree on two or three. If you have none in common, pick two from each of your lists and start there. Write your mutually selected goals in the area specified on the Profile Card inside the back cover of your handbooks.

4. *Keep a calendar and journal:* Use a calendar to schedule dates for your meetings and activities. Keep track of your progress on achieving your goals and your individual and shared accomplishments. Give praise to each other and yourself for your accomplishments. Use the Prayer and Praise Journal form in your handbooks or a journal of your own as a record of the Lord's direction and work in your relationship.

5. *Study:* Explore your Bible concordance or Bible encyclopedia. List all of the topics relating to your goals. Add any spiritual goals you may have missed. Write down all the Bible verses relating to your goals. Spend time with your mentor reading and studying these verses. Choose books to study together that will assist you with one or more of your goals.

Here is what one M&M relationship had to say about using this method of goal setting, which, incidentally, they created! It is written by Priscilla, a mentee who later became a mentor.

> Linda and I started our mentoring relationship by setting goals which we as individuals wanted to accomplish during our time together. These included: doing a weekly study, *Becoming a Woman of Prayer,* by Cynthia Heald; fun and social activities which included afternoon tea at a tea house, dinner together with our husbands, and a sports day including a golf lesson; a service project which included Easter baskets for the moms and children of the Sheepfold (a home for abused women and children); and a Mother's Day gift to the mothers at Eli Home (another home for abused women and children). P.S.: Goals accomplished!

[1] Taken from: *Between Women of God* by Donna Otto. Copyright © 1995 by Harvest House Publishers, Eugene, Oregon 97402, 46-48. Used by permission.

[2] Lucibel VanAtta, *Women Encouraging Women* (Sisters, OR: Multnomah, 1987), 137. Author's permission given. (Out of print.)

[3] Ibid, 52.

Appendix

Books That I Recommend

After the Boxes Are Unpacked: Moving on After Moving In by Susan Miller

Beloved Unbeliever by Jo Berry

Conversations with God by Lloyd John Ogilvie

Debt Free Living: How to Get Out of Debt and Stay Out by Larry Burkett

Forgiving Our Parents Forgiving Ourselves by Dr. David Stoop and James Masteller

How to Keep a Spiritual Journal by Ronald Klug

In the Company of Women by Dr. Brenda Hunter

Making Love Last Forever by Gary Smalley

My Utmost for His Highest by Oswald Chambers

Out of the Saltshaker and into the World: Evangelism as a Way of Life by Rebecca Manley Pippert

Treasured Friends: Finding and Keeping True Friendships by Ann Hibbard

When a Friend Gets a Divorce by Sharon G. Marshall

When God Doesn't Make Sense by Dr. James Dobson

A Woman's Guide to Spiritual Warfare: A Woman's Guide for Battle
by Quin Sherrer and Ruthanne Garlock

Women Home Alone: Learning to Thrive Help for Single Women, Single Moms, Widows, and Wives Who Are Frequently Alone by Patricia Sprinkle

Women Leaving the Workplace: How to Make the Transition from Work to Home by Larry Burkett

On Mentoring:

Becoming a Woman of Influence: Making a Lasting Impact on Others by Carol Kent

Between Women of God: The Gentle Art of Mentoring by Donna Otto

Connecting: Healing for Ourselves and Our Relationships a Radical New Vision by Larry Crabb

A Garden Path to Mentoring: Planting Your Life in Another and Releasing the Fragrance of Christ
by Esther Burroughs

The Gentle Art of Mentoring by Donna Otto

The Influential Woman: How Every Woman Can Make a Difference in the Lives of Other Women
by Vickie Kraft

Mentoring: Confidence in Finding a Mentor and Becoming One by Bobb Biehl

Spiritual Mothering: The Titus 2 Model for Women Mentoring Women by Susan Hunt

A Woman God Can Use: Lessons from Old Testament Women Help You Make Today's Choices
by Alice Mathews

Women Helping Women—A Biblical Guide to the Major Issues Women Face
by Elyse Fitzpatrick and Carol Cornish

Frequently Asked Questions and Suggested Answers

Question: My husband is jealous of the time we spend together. He thinks we are talking about him. How can I help him accept our relationship?

Answer: Introduce your mentor to your husband and family if you have not already done so. This way they get to know her, and she is not just someone who takes his wife or their mommy away from them.

- A husband may feel insecure if there are marital problems, and he feels you are discussing them with your mentor. This could make him feel awkward. If this is actually happening, remember that your time together with your mentor is about the two of you, and you do not want to spend your time talking about your husband. You are the only one you have control of changing in the situation, so as you draw closer to God your problems with your husband will probably become more manageable.
- When your mentor calls on the phone and your husband or kids answer, ask her to spend a moment saying "Hi" to them, and to be sure to call them by name.
- If you see your mentor at church or out in public, include your husband and the kids in the conversation. Let them know your mentor is a friend of the family. Some families do actually end up doing things together, and the husbands enjoy being included and getting to know each other.

Question: We are both so busy. We really have difficulty finding time to meet. I know we need to meet more often. How do others fit it into their schedules?

Answer: This is Satan's way of keeping you from meeting, which means that some great things are going to come about if you two get together regularly. Do not let him win. Get back in control of your time.

We all know that we make time for things that are important in our lives, and this mentoring relationship is important. So you need to make the time. We are all busy and overcommitted—no one has a corner on that. Yet some very busy women manage to meet every week faithfully because they know it is important, and what they committed to do.

Make an agreement that you will meet for only one hour every week. One week you will make a major sacrifice in your schedule, and the next week she will. By that I mean maybe one of you will have to meet the other at work at lunch time, or you will have to meet late at night after the kids are in bed, or very early in the morning for breakfast. Balance the sacrifice so it is not always one person being inconvenienced. Most importantly— pray about it. Both of you give your schedules up to God, and He will help you make the time. You can do it!

Question: What if I feel my mentor is not acting appropriately in the relationship, or is stepping over boundaries that make me uncomfortable?

Answer: If you feel your mentor is beginning to take unfair advantage of the situation or is not acting appropriately, there are several things you can do.
- Pray about the situation and ask God for wisdom to deal with it.
- Talk openly with your mentor and let her know your feelings.
- Talk to your **Prayer Warrior** and ask her advice and prayerful council.
- Call the **Ministry Relations Shepherdess** or **Ministry Leader** and ask for their help and perhaps intervention.

A mentoring relationship is meant to be a constructive and rewarding experience. You may need to go back over your goals together and redefine your relationship.

Question: My mentor is going through a crisis in her life. I feel like I might be a burden to her. Should I step out of her life and find another mentor?

Answer: Life happens to us all whether we are mentoring or not. It is pretty much a given that sometime during your relationship one of you is going to have a crisis, even if it is just a mini-crisis. If it does happen to your mentor, this is the time that you can give back to her and be there for her.

It can also be a time when you continue to learn from her. What do Christian women do in crisis? Being a Christian does not absolve us from having bad experiences or tough times. What it does do is give us a joy in our circumstances and a different way of dealing with things than the world does. Watch her and learn, because you may someday have to go through the same trial.

Question: When will I know I am ready to be a mentor myself? I think that I could help someone as my mentor has helped me. Should I try it?

Answer: How exciting that you want to give as you have been given to! Talk this over with your mentor. At this point she knows where you are spiritually and can give you a good evaluation of your readiness for mentoring. Pray about it with her and on your own. If you feel peace and you both agree that this is the next step, then go to the next Coffee. If you both determine that you are ready, be sure and read some of the mentoring books listed on the recommended book list in your handbook.

However, if you are a fairly new Christian I would suggest that you wait a few years. You might want to read a book on witnessing and begin inviting those who are spiritually younger than you to church. Wisdom comes with age and time. If you are in your 20s, you might want to consider volunteering to help the high school group in your church. A great deal of informal mentoring can take place in that environment.

Mentor and Mentee Prayer and Praise Journal

Meeting Date	Prayer Requests	Praises
	Mentor Mentee	
	Mentor Mentee	
	Mentor Mentee	
	Mentor Mentee	
	Mentor Mentee	
	Mentor Mentee	
	Mentor Mentee	
	Mentor Mentee	